Air Fryer Recipes

Cook, Grill and Bake your Everyday Healthy Foods and Snacks with this Quick and Easy Guide

© **Copyright 2017 by Charlie Baker. All rights reserved.**

ISBN-13: 978-1974205189
ISBN-10: 1974205185

In no way is it legal to reproduce, duplicate, or transmit any part of this document in either electronic means or in printed format. Recording of this publication is strictly prohibited and any storage of this document is not allowed unless with written permission from the publisher. All rights reserved.

The information provided herein is stated to be truthful and consistent, in that any liability, in terms of inattention or otherwise, by any usage or abuse of any policies, processes, or directions contained within is the solitary and utter responsibility of the recipient reader. Under no circumstances will any legal responsibility or blame be held against the author or publisher for any reparation, damages, or monetary loss due to the information herein, either directly or indirectly.

Respective authors own all copyrights not held by the publisher.

Legal Notice
This book is copyright protected. This is only for personal use. You cannot amend, distribute, sell, use, quote or paraphrase any part or the content within this book without the consent of the author or copyright owner. Legal action will be pursued if this is breached.

Disclaimer Notice
Please note the information contained within this document is for educational and entertainment purposes only. Every attempt has been made to provide accurate, up to date, and reliable complete information. No warranties of any kind are expressed or implied. Readers acknowledge that the author is not engaging in the rendering of legal, financial, medical or professional advice.

By reading this document, the reader agrees that under no circumstances are the author or publisher responsible for any losses, direct or indirect, which are incurred as a result of the use of information contained within this document, including, but not limited to errors, omissions, or inaccuracies.

Trademarks
The trademarks that are used are without any consent, and the publication of the trademark is without permission or backing by the trademark owner. All trademarks and brands within this book are for clarification purposes only, and are owned by the owners themselves, who are not affiliated with this document.

Get Our Newest Books For FREE!

We love writing about ways to improve your health.

If you want to receive a FREE COPY of any future books that we release, please sign up to our VIP list.

To show our appreciation, after confirming your subscription, you will be able to download the FREE BONUS report below.

www.restrolla.com/VIP-CoBLo

Table of Contents

Introduction 1

1. Breakfast Recipes 3
   Kale and Goat Cheese Frittata 5
   Creamy and Crispy Hash Brown and Egg Bake 7
   Bacon and Egg Toast Cups 9
   Dutch Pancake 11
   Breakfast Bacon Quiche 13

2. Lunch Recipes 15
   Mushroom Pita Pizzas 17
   Spinach Quiche 19
   English muffin Tuna Sandwiches 21
   Pesto Gnocchi 23
   Pesto Bruschetta 25

3. Meat Recipes for Dinner 27
   Chicken a La King 29
   Paprika Roast Chicken with Crispy Potato Rosti 31
   Sockeye Salmon en Papillotte with Potatoes, Fennel & Dill 33
   Homemade Sausage Rolls in an air fryer 35
   Air Fried Pork Chops 37
   Pork Chops and Potatoes 39
   Rib Eye Steak 41
   Beef Roll Up 43

4. Vegetarian Recipes for Dinner 45
   Cauliflower Veggie Burger 47
   Macaroni and Cheese Toasties 49
   Cheesy Cutlets 51
   Scalloped Potatoes 53
   Crispy Healthy Veg Rolls 55

5. Snacks and Appetizer Recipes 57
   Shrimp Croquettes 59
   Beef and Mango Skewers 61
   Crispy Grilled Spiced Cauliflower 63
   Bacon Tater Tots 65

    Buffalo Chicken Bites 67
    Grilled Salsa Roja 69

6. Side Dishes Recipes 71
    Brussels sprouts and Horseradish cream with Crispy Shallots and Bacon 73
    Roasted Vegetable Salad 75
    Cheddar Cheese Biscuits 77
    Roasted Heritage Carrots and Rhubarb 79
    Cheesy Potatoes 81

7. Dessert Recipes 83
    Peanut Butter and Jelly Banana Boat 85
    Berry Crumble 87
    Rhubarb and Strawberry Compote 89
    Apple Dumplings 91
    Soft Chocolate Chip Cookies 93
    Strawberry Jam Tarts 95

Keep Cooking Healthy Air Fryer Recipes 97

Introduction

Are you fond of fried treats?

Well, who isn't?

If your answer happens to be *yes*, then I am sure you end up feeling slightly "guilty" after eating all the fried stuff, more so if you happen to be on a diet or when you are trying to lose some weight.

What if I tell you that you can give in to your cravings and have all the fried foods you want without having to worry about the accompanying guilt or the calories? *Does this surprise you?*

Well, this is where a magical kitchen appliance known as an air fryer comes in. You can have fried food that is not only healthy but is light on calories as well! Wait a minute, fried food that is healthy? Sounds a little dubious? Well, hold on, this is true. The air fryer is indeed an excellent piece of kitchen equipment.

The latest addition to the list of really helpful and useful kitchen gadgets is an Air Fryer. Don't let its name fool you. An air fryer can do so much more than just frying food for you.

You will be able to whip up a three-course meal with an air fryer.

An air fryer makes use of hot air for cooking the food. If you are someone who has hardly any time to cook and want to eat healthy at the same time, then this is for you.

The air fryer recipes that are mentioned in this book will leave you pleasantly surprised. This air fryer recipes cookbook is segregated into different categories like breakfast, lunch, dinner, desserts, snacks, appetizers and side dishes for your convenience. You will find recipes that will chime with various diets, including paleo diets – so it's a paleo air fryer cookbook too.

An air fryer has plenty of benefits that go beyond just frying food. An air fryer will help in reducing the cooking time, cook healthier meals, cook food without any grease or oil, it is easy to clean, cost effective and it won't stink up your kitchen. It is multifunctional, and it is easy to use! You'll be making air fryer healthy recipes in no time.

The benefits it offers indeed make it a wonderful appliance. If you never thought that cooking could get much simpler, well, allow this magical appliance to change that for you. So, get started with your air fryer recipes book and enjoy great tasting food.

Happy cooking!

1. Breakfast Recipes

Kale and Goat Cheese Frittata

Serves: 1

Ingredients:

- 2 eggs
- 2 tablespoons red bell pepper, chopped
- 1 ounce goat's cheese, crumbed
- 2 tablespoons milk
- A handful kale, discard hard stems and ribs
- Salt to taste
- Pepper to taste
- 1 teaspoon olive oil

Method:

1. Add red pepper and kale into the baking accessory and stir.
2. Place the baking dish a preheated air fryer and bake at 355° F for 5 minutes.
3. Meanwhile add eggs, salt, pepper, oil and milk into a bowl and whisk well.
4. Pour the egg mixture all over vegetables in the air fryer. Spread it evenly.
5. Bake for 3 minutes. Sprinkle goat's cheese and bake for 2 more minutes.
6. Carefully slide the frittata on to the serving plate. Slice into wedges and serve.

Creamy and Crispy Hash Brown and Egg Bake

Serves: 1-2

Ingredients:

- 2 cups refrigerated hash browns, divided
- 1 cup cheese, shredded (optional)
- 2 large eggs, lightly beaten
- ½ teaspoon all-purpose seasoning blend or to taste
- Salt to taste
- Pepper to taste
- 5 ¼ ounces cream of potato soup or any other cream style soup
- ½ cup mixed vegetables of your choice, cooked
- 1 tablespoon olive oil
- Cooking spray

Method:

1. Grease the baking accessory with cooking spray. Add 1-cup hash browns and spread it all over the dish. Press it lightly.
2. Pour soup over the hash browns. Swirl the dish so that the soup spreads evenly.
3. Sprinkle vegetables and cheese if using.
4. Beat eggs lightly and pour into the dish. Spread the remaining hash browns over it.
5. Sprinkle salt, pepper, seasoning blend and oil over it.

7. Place the baking dish a preheated air fryer and bake at 355° F for 20-30 minutes or until the top is brown.
6. Remove from the air fryer and cool for a few minutes.
7. Cut into wedges and serve.

Bacon and Egg Toast Cups

Serves: 2

Ingredients:

- 1 slice bread, remove crust, halved
- 2 eggs
- 2 strips bacon, cooked
- Salt to taste
- Pepper to taste

Method:

1. Grease 2 muffin cups with cooking spray and set aside.
2. Place each half of the bread slice into the muffin cup. Press it onto the bottom as well as the sides.
3. Place the bacon slices around the edges of the muffin cups. Break an egg into each cup.
4. Place the muffin cups in the air fryer basket.
5. Air fry in a preheated air fryer at 390° F for about 8-10 minutes or until the eggs are set.
6. Remove from the oven and set aside to cool. Run a knife around the edges of the muffin cups and carefully slide on to a plate.
7. Serve hot or warm.

Dutch Pancake

Serves: 2

Ingredients:

- 2 small eggs
- 1 tablespoon butter, unsalted
- ¼ cup flour
- ¼ teaspoon vanilla extract
- 1 tablespoon powdered sugar
- ¼ cup milk
- ¾ cup fresh strawberries, sliced

Method:

1. Place the baking accessory in the air fryer basket and preheat the air fryer to 350° F. Add butter into it. When butter melts, remove the pan from the air fryer.
2. Swirl the pan so that the butter spreads all over pan.
3. Add flour, eggs, milk and vanilla into a bowl and whisk until frothy. Pour into the pan.
8. Place the pan in the air fryer basket. Bake in a preheated air fryer at 350° F for about 12-16 minutes or until the pancake is golden brown.
9. Remove from the oven and set aside to cool. Run a knife around the edges of the pancake and carefully slide on to a plate.
10. Sprinkle strawberry slices and powdered sugar on the pancake. Cut into 2 halves
11. Serve hot or warm.

Breakfast Bacon Quiche

Serves: 3

Ingredients:

- 1 medium refrigerated pie crust
- 1 ½ cups Colby and Monterey Jack cheese blend, shredded
- 6 tablespoon sour cream
- Salt to taste
- Pepper to taste
- ½ pound bacon, cooked, crumbled
- 3 large eggs
- 1 small green bell pepper, chopped

Method:

1. Spray a small round baking pan with cooking spray. Place the piecrust in it.
2. Place the pan in the air fryer basket.
3. Bake in a preheated air fryer at 350° F for 5 minutes.
4. Remove the pan from the air fryer.
5. Sprinkle half the bacon, bell pepper and cheese over the piecrust.
6. Add eggs and sour cream into a bowl. Whisk well. Add salt and pepper and whisk again. Pour over the crust.
7. Place the pan back into the air fryer.
8. Bake in a preheated air fryer at 350° F for 12-15 minutes or until the center is set.
9. Sprinkle remaining bacon on it. Slice into wedges and serve.

2. Lunch Recipes

Mushroom Pita Pizzas

Serves: 1

Ingredients:

- 2 pitas (3 inches each)
- 6 tablespoons pizza sauce
- ¼ teaspoon dried basil
- ½ cup mozzarella or provolone cheese, grated
- ½ tablespoon olive oil
- 2 ounces jarred, mushrooms, drained, sliced
- 1 green onion, thinly sliced
- ½ cup grape tomatoes, sliced

Method:

1. Brush the pitas with olive oil.
2. Spread pizza sauce over it. Place mushroom slices all over the pitas. Sprinkle basil and green onions.
3. Sprinkle cheese right on top.
4. Bake in a preheated air fryer at 350° F for about 3-6 minutes or until the cheese melts and is browned at a few spots.
5. Remove from the air fryer. Place grape tomatoes on top and serve right away.

Spinach Quiche

Serves: 2

Ingredients:

- 2 eggs
- 1 tablespoons heavy cream
- 2/3 cup frozen spinach, thawed, drained
- 2 teaspoons honey mustard sauce
- ½ teaspoon dried thyme
- Freshly ground pepper to taste
- Salt to taste
- 1/3 cup Swiss cheese, grated
- A little flour to dust

Method:

1. Add eggs into a bowl and whisk well. Add, honey mustard, cream, salt and pepper and whisk well.
2. Add spinach, cheese and thyme. Mix well.
3. Spray the baking accessory with cooking spray. Dust with a little flour.
4. Pour the entire mixture into the pan. Place the pan in the air fryer.
5. Bake in a preheated air fryer at 350° F for about 15-20 minutes or until set and is browned at a few spots.
6. Cool for 5 minutes. Slice into wedges and serve.

English muffin Tuna Sandwiches

Serves: 2

Ingredients:

- 3 ounces canned chunk light tuna, drained
- 1 tablespoon mustard
- 1 green onion, minced
- 2 English muffins
- 4 thin slices provolone cheese or Muenster cheese
- 4 teaspoons butter, softened
- 2 tablespoons mayonnaise
- 2 teaspoons lemon juice

Method:

1. Preheat the air fryer to 350° F.
2. Add tuna, mustard, mayonnaise, green onions and lemon juice into a bowl. Mix well.
3. Split the English muffins. Spread butter on the cut part of the muffins.
4. Place in the air fryer with the buttered side facing up.
5. Grill for 2-4 minutes or until the top is light brown in color.
6. Place a slice of cheese on each half of the muffin. Air fry for a couple of minutes until the cheese melts.
7. Remove the muffins from the air fryer and place on your work area. Divide the tuna mixture and spread on top of the muffins.
8. Serve right away.

Pesto Gnocchi

Serves: 2

Ingredients:

- 1 ½ teaspoons olive oil
- 2 cloves garlic, minced
- 4 ounces pesto
- 8 ounces package shelf stable gnocchi
- 3 tablespoons parmesan cheese, grated
- 1 small onion, finely chopped

Method:

1. Add oil, garlic, onion and gnocchi into the air fryer baking accessory.
2. Bake in a preheated air fryer at 350° F for about 15-20 minutes or until light brown and crisp. Stir the contents half way through baking.
3. Add pesto and cheese and stir.
4. Serve right away.

Pesto Bruschetta

Serves: 2

Ingredients:

- 4 slices baguette (½ inch thickness of each slice)
- ½ cup mozzarella cheese, shredded
- Salt to taste
- Pepper to taste
- 1 tablespoon butter
- ¼ cup basil pesto
- ½ cup grape tomatoes, chopped
- 1 green onion, thinly sliced

Method:

1. Spread butter on one side of the bread slices. Place the baguette slices on the baking tray with the buttered side up.
2. Bake in a preheated air fryer at 350° F for about 8-10 minutes or until toasted to light brown. Check after about 5-6 minutes of baking. Remove the bread slices if it is ready.
3. Sprinkle cheese over the slices. Place it back in the air fryer.
4. Bake for a couple of minutes until the cheese is melted.
5. Meanwhile mix together in a bowl rest of the ingredients.
6. Spread it over the bread slices.
7. Serve immediately.

3. Meat Recipes for Dinner

Chicken a La King

Serves: 2

Ingredients:

- 1 chicken breast, skinless, boneless, chopped into 1 inch cubes
- ½ red bell pepper, chopped
- 5 ounces package refrigerated Alfredo sauce
- French bread slices to serve
- Butter, as required
- 4 button mushrooms, sliced
- ½ tablespoon olive oil
- ¼ teaspoon dried thyme

Method:

1. Add chicken, bell pepper and mushroom slices into a bowl. Drizzle oil over it. Toss well and transfer into the air fryer basket.
2. Roast in a preheated air fryer at 350° F for about 10-15 minutes or until the meat thermometer when inserted in the meat shows 165° F.
3. Transfer into the baking accessory. Add Alfredo sauce and thyme. Mix well and add it back into the air fryer.
4. Roast for 3-4 minutes. Remove the baking dish from the air fryer.
5. Lightly butter the bread slices and place in the air fryer basket.
6. Bake until light brown.

7. Place the bread slices on a serving plate. Spoon the chicken mixture over it.
8. Serve immediately.

Paprika Roast Chicken with Crispy Potato Rosti

Serves: 1

Ingredients:

- 1 chicken leg
- ¼ teaspoon garlic powder or minced fresh garlic
- 1 teaspoon smoked paprika
- Salt to taste
- Pepper to taste
- ½ teaspoon honey

For the rosti:

- 1 medium sweet potatoes, peeled, grated
- 1 small egg
- 1/8 Savoy cabbage, thinly sliced
- ½ tablespoon flour
- Freshly ground black pepper to taste
- Salt to taste
- 1 teaspoon olive oil
- 1 teaspoon fresh parsley, minced

Method:

1. Add honey, paprika, garlic powder, salt and pepper into a bowl and stir.
2. Make a few cuts on the chicken. Rub the paprika mixture into it.
3. Place the chicken in the air fryer basket.

4. Air fry at 390°F for 35 minutes or until golden brown and crisp. Turn the chicken once half way through cooking.
5. Place the chicken on a plate that is covered with foil.
6. Meanwhile make the rosti as follows: Place the grated sweet potato over kitchen a towel for a while so that it dries. Transfer into a bowl. Add cabbage, egg, salt, flour, pepper and parsley. Shape into a patty.
7. Brush the patty with oil and place in the air fryer basket.
8. Air fry for 8 minutes. Flip sides half way through cooking.
9. To serve: Place chicken leg on a serving plate. Place rosti alongside.
10. Serve with a salad of your choice.

Sockeye Salmon en Papillotte with Potatoes, Fennel & Dill

Serves: 4

Ingredients:

- 1-2 fingerling potatoes, sliced into ¼ inch thick slices
- 2 tablespoons butter, melted
- ¼ bulb fennel, sliced into ¼ inch thick slices
- Freshly ground pepper to taste
- Salt to taste
- 1 sockeye salmon fillet (6 ounces)
- 2 tablespoons dry vermouth or white wine or fish stock
- 1 tablespoon fresh dill, chopped
- 4-5 cherry tomatoes, halved

Method:

1. Place a small saucepan with water over medium heat. Add salt and potatoes. Blanch the potatoes for 2 minutes. Drain and pat the potatoes dry.
2. Add potatoes, half the butter, fennel, salt and pepper into a bowl and toss well.
3. Place a large rectangle of parchment paper on your work area. Place the potato mixture over it.
4. Sprinkle dill and place the fillet over the potatoes. Sprinkle salt and pepper over the fillet.
5. Place cherry tomatoes over the fillet. Pour the remaining butter over the tomatoes.

6. Fold the parchment paper over the fillets to make into a packet.
7. Place the packet in the air fryer.
8. Air fry in a preheated air fryer at 400° F for about 10 minutes.
9. Unwrap. Garnish with dill and serve.

Homemade Sausage Rolls in an air fryer

Serves: 2

Ingredients:

- 1 cup all-purpose flour
- ½ tablespoon olive oil
- 1 small egg, beaten
- ½ teaspoon dried parsley
- 1/3 pound sausage meat
- 3 ½ tablespoons butter
- ½ teaspoon mustard
- Salt to taste
- Pepper to taste

Method:

1. To make the pastry dough: Add flour, salt, pepper and parsley into a bowl. Add butter and mix well using your hands until a crumbly mixture is formed.
2. Add oil and mix again. Add water, a little at a time and mix with your hands to form dough. Knead into smooth dough.
3. Place the dough on your work area. Roll into a square with a rolling pin to about 1-2 mm thickness.
4. Spread the mustard all over the rolled dough. Place the sausage meat along the center of the dough. Brush egg on the edges of the pastry.

5. Roll the pastry and press lightly to seal the edges. Take a sharp knife and cut the roll into 2 equal portions.
6. Brush egg all over the roll. Make 2-3 small slits on the top of the roll.
7. Bake in a preheated air fryer at 320°F for 20 minutes. Then increase the temperature to 390°F and bake for 5 minutes.
8. Serve.

Air Fried Pork Chops

Serves: 2

Ingredients:

- 2 pork loin chops (¾ inch thick)
- ¼ cup Italian bread crumbs
- ¼ cup Dijon mustard
- ½ teaspoon pepper powder
- ½ teaspoon salt
- ¼ teaspoon cayenne pepper
- Cooking spray

Method:

1. Spread generously Dijon mustard over the pork chops.
2. Add breadcrumbs, salt, pepper and cayenne pepper into a bowl and mix well.
3. Roll the pork chops in the breadcrumbs mixture and place in the baking accessory. Spray with cooking spray.
4. Place the baking accessory in the air fryer basket.
5. Bake in a preheated air fryer at 320°F for 20 minutes or until nearly done. Then increase the temperature to 390°F and bake for 5 minutes.

Pork Chops and Potatoes

Serves: 2

Ingredients:

- 2 pork chops
- 3 small potatoes, chopped
- 1 tablespoon butter, melted
- 6 tablespoons water, divided
- ½ can cream of mushroom soup
- 1 tablespoon olive oil
- 1 cup seasoned bread crumbs
- Salt to taste
- Pepper to taste

Method:

1. Sprinkle salt and pepper over the pork chops. Place in the baking accessory.
2. Add butter, breadcrumbs and 2 tablespoons water into a bowl and mix well. Spread this mixture over the pork chops. Place the potatoes over the pork chops.
3. Mix together 2 tablespoons water and cream of mushroom soup over it.
4. Place the baking accessory in the air fryer.
5. Bake in a preheated air fryer at 350°F for 20-30 minutes or until tender.

40

Rib Eye Steak

Serves: 2

Ingredients:

- 1 pound rib eye steak
- ½ tablespoon olive oil
- ½ tablespoon steak rub

Method:

1. Sprinkle oil and rub over the steak. Rub it well into the steak.
2. Place the steak in the air fryer basket.
3. Bake in a preheated air fryer at 390°F for 15-20 minutes.

Beef Roll Up

Serves: 2

Ingredients:

- 1 pound beef flank steak
- 1 ½ tablespoons pesto or more to taste
- 1.5 ounces red bell peppers, roasted
- ½ teaspoon pepper powder
- ½ teaspoon sea salt
- 3 slices Provolone cheese
- ½ cup fresh baby spinach

Method:

1. Open the steak. Apply pesto on the opened part.
2. Place the cheese slices over it (up to ¾ the steak). Layer with roasted red peppers and spinach.
3. Roll the steak and fasten with toothpicks. Sprinkle salt and pepper over it.
4. Place the beef rollups in the air fryer basket.
5. Bake in a preheated air fryer at 390°F for 15-20 minutes or until done.
6. Turn the roll up half way through baking.
7. When done, remove from the air fryer and let it sit for 10 minutes.
8. Slice and serve.

4. Vegetarian Recipes for Dinner

Cauliflower Veggie Burger

Serves: 4

Ingredients:

- 1.1 pounds cauliflower, grated
- 1 teaspoon garlic paste
- 2 tablespoons desiccated coconut
- 1 ½ tablespoons flour
- 1 cup herb bread crumbs
- ½ cup plain bread crumbs
- 1 teaspoon dried thyme
- 1 ½ teaspoons coconut oil
- ¼ cup oats
- 1 small egg, beaten
- ½ teaspoon mustard powder
- 1 teaspoon fresh parsley, chopped
- ½ teaspoon mixed spice
- 1 teaspoon chives
- Salt to taste
- Pepper to taste

Method:

1. Steam the cauliflower in your steaming apparatus. Drain for a while in a colander. Squeeze out moisture from the cauliflower.

2. Add cauliflower into the food processor. Also add salt, pepper, garlic and mustard and blend until well combined.
3. Add salt, pepper, seasoning, coconut oil and breadcrumbs and mix well.
4. Dust your hands with flour and shape the mixture into patties.
5. Place flour in a bowl. Add herb breadcrumbs into another bowl. Add beaten egg into a third bowl.
6. First dredge patties in the bowl of flour. Next dip in the bowl of egg. Shake to drop off the excess egg. Finally dredge in herb breadcrumbs.
7. Grease a sheet of aluminum foil with a little oil.
8. Place a foil in the air fryer basket. Place the patties in it.
9. Air fry in a preheated air fryer 390°F for 15-20 minutes or until golden brown in color.
10. Serve in burger buns with toppings of your choice.

Macaroni and Cheese Toasties

Serves: 2

Ingredients:

- 4 slices bread
- ½ cup macaroni and cheese or more if required
- Cheddar cheese, grated, as required
- 1 large egg, beaten
- Salt to taste
- Pepper to taste

Method:

1. Spread macaroni and cheese evenly over 2 of the bread slices.
2. Cover with the remaining 2 slices of bread.
3. Add salt and pepper to the beaten egg and whisk well.
4. Cut the sandwiches into 2 triangles.
5. Grease a sheet of aluminum foil with a little oil.
6. Place the foil in the air fryer basket. Brush the sandwiches with beaten egg.
7. Place the sandwiches in it.
8. Air fry in a preheated air fryer 355°F for 15-20 minutes or until golden brown in color.

Cheesy Cutlets

Serves: 2

Ingredients:

- 1 cup cottage cheese, grated
- 1 small onion, finely chopped
- ½ cup mozzarella cheese, grated
- ¼ teaspoon garlic powder
- 1 teaspoon dried oregano
- Salt to taste
- ¼ teaspoon red chili flakes
- 2 tablespoons bread crumbs

Method:

1. Add all the ingredients into a bowl. Divide the mixture into 4 equal portions and shape into cutlets.
2. Grease a sheet of aluminum foil with a little oil.
3. Place the foil in the air fryer basket. Place the patties in it.
4. Air fry in a preheated air fryer 355°F for 10-12 minutes or until golden brown in color.
5. Serve with a dip of your choice.

Scalloped Potatoes

Serves: 2

Ingredients:

- 2 large baking potatoes, thinly sliced
- 2.5 ounces cream of mushroom soup
- Garlic salt to taste
- Pepper to taste
- ¼ cup sautéed mushrooms
- 2 green onions, sliced
- ¼ cup cheddar cheese, shredded, divided
- 2 tablespoons butter

Method:

1. Place potato slices in the baking accessory.
2. Bake in a preheated air fryer at 355°F for 10 minutes.
3. When done, transfer the potatoes into 2 ramekins.
4. Mix together rest of the ingredients (retain half the cheese) in a bowl.
5. Pour over the potatoes. Sprinkle remaining cheese over it.
6. Bake in a preheated air fryer at 390°F for 10 minutes.

Crispy Healthy Veg Rolls

Serves: 2-3

Ingredients:

For dough:

- 1 ½ cups flour
- ½ teaspoon salt
- 1 teaspoon oregano
- ½ teaspoon baking powder
- 1 teaspoon oil

For filling:

- 2 tablespoons bell pepper, finely chopped
- 1 large boiled potato, peeled, mashed
- 1 small bell pepper, finely chopped
- ½ teaspoon ginger paste
- ½ teaspoon garlic paste
- 1 teaspoon butter
- 1 small onion, chopped
- ¼ cup frozen peas, boiled
- 1 small carrot, grated
- 5-6 string beans, finely chopped
- 1 tablespoon frozen corn, thawed
- ¼ teaspoon chili powder
- ½ teaspoon salt
- 1 teaspoon Italian seasoning or any seasoning of your choice
- 1 tablespoon fresh parsley, finely chopped

For coating:

- 2 tablespoons cornstarch mixed with ½ cup water
- ½ cup bread crumbs

Method:

1. To make the dough: Add all the ingredients of the dough into a bowl. Add enough water and mix to form soft dough. Cover with a lid. Set aside for 2 hours.
2. Meanwhile make filling as follows: Place a skillet over medium heat. Add butter. When butter melts, add onions and sauté until translucent.
3. Add ginger paste and garlic paste. Sauté for a couple of minutes until fragrant.
4. Add bell pepper, beans, carrot and corn. Sauté for a few minutes until the vegetables are tender.
5. Add chili powder, salt, seasoning and potatoes and cook until the mixture is thoroughly heated. Add parsley and mix.
6. Remove from heat and set aside to cool.
7. Place cornstarch mixed with water in a bowl. Place bread crumbs on a plate.
8. Make small balls of the dough. Place the balls on your work area. Roll each of the balls with a rolling pin.
9. Place some of the filling in the center of the rolled dough and fold over to roll. Seal the edges firmly.
10. Dip the rolls in the corn flour mixture and then dredge in the breadcrumbs.
11. Place in the air fryer basket.
12. Air fry in a preheated air fryer at 390°F for 15 minutes or until golden brown.
13. Serve with hot sauce or ketchup or green chutney.

5. Snacks and Appetizer Recipes

Shrimp Croquettes

Serves: 1-2

Ingredients:

- 1/3 pound shrimp, peeled, deveined, cooked, minced
- 1 small egg, beaten
- 1 green onion, finely chopped
- Salt to taste
- Freshly ground pepper to taste
- ¾ cup bread crumbs, divided
- 1 tablespoon lemon juice
- ¼ teaspoon dried basil
- 1 tablespoon olive oil

Method:

1. Add half the breadcrumbs, lemon juice and egg into a bowl. Mix well and set aside for 5 minutes.
2. Add shrimp, basil, green onion, pepper and salt into it. Mix well.
3. Divide the mixture into 3-4 equal portions and shape into croquettes.
4. Add remaining breadcrumbs and oil into a shallow bowl. Mix well.
5. Dredge the croquettes in the breadcrumb mixture and place in the air fryer basket.
6. Air fry in a preheated air fryer 355°F for 10-12 minutes or until golden brown in color.
7. Serve with a dip of your choice.

Beef and Mango Skewers

Serves: 2

Ingredients:

- ½ pound beef sirloin, cut into 1 inch cubes
- 1 ½ teaspoons oil
- 1 tablespoon balsamic vinegar
- 2 teaspoons honey
- Freshly ground pepper to taste
- Salt to taste
- ½ teaspoon dried marjoram
- 1 ripe, firm mango, peeled, cut into 1 ½ inch cubes

Method:

1. Add vinegar, honey, oil, marjoram, salt and pepper into a bowl. Mix well.
2. Add beef cubes and mix well. Rub the marinade into the beef cubes with your hands. Set aside for 30 minutes.
3. Thread the beef cubes and mango cubes on to metal skewers.
4. Place the skewers in the air fryer basket.
5. Grill in a preheated air fryer 355°F for 4-7 minutes or until done.

Crispy Grilled Spiced Cauliflower

Serves: 4

Ingredients:

- 1 large cauliflower head
- 2 eggs, beaten
- ½ cup bread crumbs

For the spice mixture:

- Salt to taste
- Freshly ground pepper powder to taste
- ½ teaspoon ground turmeric
- ¼ teaspoon ground coriander
- ¼ teaspoon ground cumin
- ½ teaspoon crushed red pepper
- ¼ teaspoon garlic powder
- ¼ teaspoon ginger powder

Method:

1. Place a large pot filled with water over high heat. Add about a teaspoon of salt.
2. When water begins to boil, add cauliflower and boil for 3 - 4 minutes until cauliflower is slightly tender.
3. Remove from the water with a slotted spoon and pat dry the cauliflower. Chop into florets.
4. Add the spice mixture to the cauliflower and toss well.

5. Add a little salt and pepper to beaten egg.
6. Dip cauliflower in the egg mixture. Shake off the excess egg. Then dredge in breadcrumbs and place it in the air fryer basket. Bake in batches if required.
7. Air fry in a preheated air fryer at 355°F for 15 minutes.
8. Serve hot.

Bacon Tater Tots

Serves: 4

Ingredients: 2

- 1 dozen frozen tater tots
- 1 tablespoon maple syrup
- 3 slices precooked bacon, chopped into 1 inch pieces (do not use regular bacon, use precooked and non-refrigerated bacon)
- ½ cup cheddar cheese, shredded

Method:

1. Place tater tots in the air fryer basket.
2. Air fry in a preheated air fryer at 390°F for 10 minutes. Shake the basket half way through cooking.
3. Transfer tater tots into the baking accessory. Add bacon and maple syrup and toss well. Place the baking accessory in the air fryer basket.
4. Air fry for 5 minutes or until crisp.
5. Sprinkle cheese. Air fry for 2 minutes or until the cheese melts.

Buffalo Chicken Bites

Serves: 2

Ingredients:

- 1/3 cup sour cream
- 2 tablespoons blue cheese, crumbled
- ½ pound chicken tenders, cut into thirds, crosswise
- ½ cup panko bread crumbs
- 2 tablespoons creamy blue cheese salad dressing
- 1 small stalk celery, finely chopped
- 4 teaspoons Buffalo chicken wing sauce
- 1 tablespoon olive oil

Method:

1. Add sour cream, blue cheese, blue cheese salad dressing and celery into a bowl. Mix well. Set aside for a while for the flavors to set in.
2. Add chicken and buffalo wing sauce into a bowl. Toss well.
3. Add breadcrumbs and olive oil in a shallow wide bowl.
4. Dredge the chicken pieces in the breadcrumb mixture and place in the air fryer basket. Air fry in bathes if required.
5. Air fry in a preheated air fryer at 355°F for 12-15 minutes or until golden brown. Shake the basket half way through cooking.
6. Serve with blue cheese sauce.

Grilled Salsa Roja

Serves: 4

Ingredients:

- 4 plum tomatoes, cored
- 2 Serrano chilies
- ½ cup packed fresh cilantro leaves with tender stems
- 1 small white onion, peeled, halved
- 2 cloves garlic, peeled
- Salt to taste

Method:

1. Place the grilling accessory in the air fryer.
2. Add tomatoes, chilies and onion into the grilling accessory.
3. Grill in a preheated air fryer at 390°F for about 10 minutes or until lightly charred.
4. Check after every 2-3 minutes of cooking. The cooking time varies for all the 3 vegetables. Remove the vegetable that gets charred first and add into a bowl. Then remove the vegetable that gets charred next and add into the bowl. Finally the last vegetable to get charred and add into the bowl.
5. When cool enough to handle, transfer into a blender.
6. Add garlic, salt and cilantro. Blend until smooth. Transfer into a bowl. Cover and refrigerate until use.
7. Serve with fresh vegetable sticks. You can also use it as a dip with your favorite snack.

6. Side Dishes Recipes

Brussels sprouts and Horseradish cream with Crispy Shallots and Bacon

Serves: 1

Ingredients:

- ¾ pound Brussels sprouts, halved lengthwise
- ½ cup thick cut bacon, diced
- ½ tablespoon olive oil
- 1 tablespoon butter
- ¼ cup milk
- 1 tablespoon prepared horseradish
- A pinch ground nutmeg
- Salt to taste
- Freshly ground pepper to taste
- 1 shallot, sliced
- 1 tablespoon flour
- ½ cup heavy cream
- 1 teaspoon fresh thyme leaves

Method:

1. Add Brussels sprouts into a bowl. Season with salt and pepper and toss well. Transfer on to the baking accessory.
1. Place in the air fryer basket.
2. Air fry in a preheated air fryer at 390°F for about 8-10 minutes or until brown and crisp. Check the Brussels

sprouts after 5 minutes of cooking. Shake the basket each time you check the Brussels sprouts. Remove from the air fryer when done and add into the baking accessory.
3. Add bacon into the air fryer basket. Pour a little water in the drawer below to catch the drippings.
4. Air fry for 8-10 minutes. Shake the basket a couple of times while it is frying.
5. Add shallots and mix well.
6. Continue frying for another 10-15 minutes until the bacon begins to get light brown and the shallots soften. Sprinkle salt and pepper and toss well.
7. Transfer on to a plate that is lined with a couple of layers of paper towels. Set aside for a few minutes.
8. Meanwhile, place a saucepan over medium heat. Add butter. When butter melts, add flour, whisking constantly. Sauté for a few seconds until fragrant.
9. Add milk and cream, whisking constantly. Simmer until the mixture is thick. Keep stirring all the while.
10. Add horseradish, nutmeg, thyme and salt. Mix well and remove from heat. Pour into the dish of Brussels sprouts. Spread it all over the Brussels sprouts. But do not stir.
11. Sprinkle bacon and shallot mixture.
12. Place the baking accessory in the air fryer.
13. Bake in a preheated air fryer at 350°F for about 8-10 minutes.
14. Serve hot.

Roasted Vegetable Salad

Serves: 2-3

Ingredients:

- 2 parsnips, peeled, chopped into bite sized cubes
- 1 butternut squash, deseeded, chopped into bite sized cubes
- 2 celeriac's, peeled, chopped into bite sized cubes
- 1 large carrot, peeled, chopped into bite sized cubes
- 1 medium yellow bell pepper, cut into 1 inch squares
- 1 medium red bell pepper, cut into 1 inch squares
- 1 medium zucchini, cut into ½ inch thick slices
- 1 onion, chopped into wedges
- 1 tablespoon fresh thyme, chopped
- 2 teaspoons olive oil
- ¼ teaspoon cayenne pepper (optional)
- Salt to taste
- Pepper powder to taste
- ½ cup fresh mint leaves, torn

Method:

1. Add all the vegetables except mint into a bowl. Add thyme, oil, salt, pepper and cayenne pepper. Toss well.
2. Transfer the vegetables in the air fryer basket.
3. Roast in a preheated air fryer at 390°F for 20 minutes or until golden brown.
4. Remove from the air fryer and stir in the mint leaves.
5. Serve hot.

Cheddar Cheese Biscuits

Serves: 4

Ingredients:

- 1 cup + 3 tablespoons self raising flour
- ½ cup all purpose flour, for shaping
- ¼ cup butter, frozen for 15 minutes
- 2/3 cup buttermilk
- ½ tablespoon butter, melted
- 1 tablespoon sugar
- ¼ cup cheddar cheese, grated + extra to top

Method:

1. Line the baking accessory with parchment paper or silicone liner and set aside.
2. Add self-raising flour and sugar into a mixing bowl. Grate the frozen butter and add into the mixing bowl.
3. Add cheese and mix well with your hands until the mixture is crumbly.
4. Add buttermilk and mix until soft, wet dough is formed.
5. Take a cookie sheet and sprinkle some of the all-purpose flour on it.
6. Divide the mixture into 4 portions and scoop each portion on the cookie sheet.
7. Coat your hands with flour and coat each scoop of dough in flour.

8. Toss the dough between your hands a couple of times and place in the prepared baking accessory. Place it close to each other.
9. Place the baking accessory in the air fryer.
10. Bake in a preheated air fryer at 380°F for 20 minutes or until light brown. A toothpick when inserted in the center should come out clean. But keep a watch on the biscuits after about 12-13 minutes of baking.
11. Brush melted butter on the top. Sprinkle cheese on top.
12. Air fry for another 2-3 minutes or until the cheese melts.
13. Remove from the air fryer and cool for a couple of minutes. Pull apart and serve.

Roasted Heritage Carrots and Rhubarb

Serves: 2

Ingredients:

- 1 teaspoon walnut oil
- ½ pound rhubarb, chop into chunks
- ½ pound heritage carrots, chop into chunks
- ¼ teaspoon stevia
- 1 small orange, peeled, separated into segments
- Zest of an orange, grated
- ¼ cup walnuts, chopped

Method:

1. Add carrots into the baking accessory. Drizzle oil over it and toss.
2. Roast in a preheated air fryer at 320°F for 20 minutes.
3. Increase the temperature to at 350°F and roast for 6 minutes.
4. Add rhubarb, stevia and walnuts. Toss again.
5. Roast for 6 minutes.
6. Add zest and oranges and toss well.
7. Serve immediately.

Cheesy Potatoes

Serves: 3

Ingredients:

- 3 potatoes, sliced
- 1 tablespoon cold butter or margarine
- 6 tablespoons mozzarella cheese, shredded
- 2 tablespoons parmesan cheese, grated
- 6 tablespoons cheddar cheese, shredded
- Salt to taste
- Pepper to taste

Method:

1. Spray the baking accessory with cooking spray. Add all the ingredients into the baking accessory. Mix well. Spread it all over the pan.
2. Bake in a preheated air fryer at 330°F for 20 minutes or until the potatoes are tender.
3. Serve hot.

82

7. Dessert Recipes

Peanut Butter and Jelly Banana Boat

Serves: 2-3

Ingredients:

- 2 bananas, peeled
- ½ cup jelly or to taste
- ½ cup peanut butter
- 2 tablespoons granola

Method:

1. Slit the banana along the length up to ¾ (do not cut into 2 halves)
2. Take 2 sheets of tin foil. Shape each into a cradle (the size should be as big as the banana). Place the bananas in each tin foil.
3. Slightly open the slit banana. Spread peanut butter and jelly in the opened part.
4. Sprinkle granola over it.
5. Place the bananas in the air fryer basket.
6. Bake in a preheated air fryer at 330°F for 15-20 minutes.
7. Remove from the air fryer and serve warm.

Berry Crumble

Serves: 8-10

Ingredients:

- 1 ½ cups +6 tablespoons flour
- 1/8 teaspoon ground cinnamon
- 1/8 teaspoon ground nutmeg
- 1/8 teaspoon ground cloves
- 1/8 teaspoon ground ginger
- ½ cup butter, chilled, chopped into small cubes
- ¾ tablespoon baking powder
- 1 cup + 2 tablespoons sugar
- ½ teaspoon salt
- 1 ½ pounds berries of your choice

Method:

1. Add flour, salt, spices and baking powder into the food processor bowl. Pulse until well combined.
2. Add butter and pulse until well combined. Add sugar and pulse again until the mixture is well combined and crumbly in texture.
3. Take 2 baking dishes that fit well in the air fryer.
4. Sprinkle half the berries in each. Sprinkle half the flour mixture on top of the berries in each dish. Bake in batches.
5. Bake in a preheated air fryer at 330°F for 15-20 minutes.
6. Remove from the air fryer. Cool for a while and serve warm.

Rhubarb and Strawberry Compote

Serves: 4

Ingredients:

- ¼ pound strawberries, hulled, chopped
- ¼ pound rhubarb stalk, sliced
- 1-2 tablespoons honey
- ½ teaspoon orange zest, grated
- 2 tablespoons orange juice

Method:

1. Add strawberries, rhubarb, honey, orange juice and zest into the baking accessory. Toss well.
2. Roast in a preheated air fryer at 375°F for 20-30 minutes or until tender. Stir a couple of times while it is roasting.
3. The compote should be thick in consistency.
4. Serve at room temperature. You can also top it over cakes or ice cream and serve.

Apple Dumplings

Serves: 2

Ingredients:

- 2 apples, cored up to ¾
- 2 tablespoons butter, softened
- ½ teaspoon apple pie spice
- 2 tablespoons brown sugar
- 1 tablespoon walnuts, chopped
- 2 discs refrigerated pie dough
- 1 beaten egg (optional)

Method:

1. Mix together in a bowl, butter, walnuts brown sugar and apple pie spice. Stuff this mixture into the core of the apples.
2. Take the pie dough and place on your work area. (If the disc is very big, then cut into 2 halves and use) Place the stuffed apple over it. Bring the edges of the dough and enclose the apple completely. Brush with egg is using. Place in the air fryer basket.
3. Grill in a preheated air fryer at 350°F for 20 -30 minutes or until light brown on top.
4. Remove from the air fryer. Cool for a while and serve warm.

Soft Chocolate Chip Cookies

Serves: 6

Ingredients:

- 4.5 ounces self raising flour
- 3 tablespoons brown sugar
- 1 ½ tablespoons coconut sugar
- 5 tablespoons butter
- 1 ½ tablespoons whole milk
- ½ teaspoon vanilla extract
- ½ cup chocolate chips, crushed or chopped
- 2 tablespoons honey
- ½ tablespoon cocoa powder

Method:

1. Add butter and sugar into a mixing bowl. Beat using an electric mixer until light and creamy.
2. Add flour, milk, cocoa, honey and vanilla. Mix well using a fork.
3. Coat your hands with a little flour. Add chocolate chips and mix well using your hands.
4. Divide the mixture into 6 equal portions.
5. Line the air fryer basket with foil. Roll the cookies and place in the air fryer.
6. Bake in a preheated air fryer at 390°F for 15 minutes.
7. Remove from the air fryer. Cool for a while and serve.

Strawberry Jam Tarts

Serves: 4

Ingredients:

- 1 cup flour
- 2 tablespoons caster sugar
- 3 tablespoons butter
- Strawberry jam, as required
- Water, as required

Method:

1. Add flour, sugar and butter into a bowl. Mix well using your hands until crumbly.
2. Add enough water and form into firm dough.
3. Grease 4 small pastry cases. Divide and place the dough in each case. Press it on to the bottom as well as the sides.
4. Spread a little jam on the bottom of pastry dough in the cases. Place the tarts in the air fryer basket.
5. Bake in a preheated air fryer at 355°F for 15 minutes.
6. Remove from the air fryer. Cool for a while and serve.

Keep Cooking Healthy Air Fryer Recipes

An Air Fryer is an excellent kitchen appliance and makes use of hot air for frying foods without any oil or fat. This is great news for all home cooks who enjoy the flavor and the textures of deep fried foods but aren't fond of all the accompanying fat and calories - not to mention the trouble of having to clean up the mess after deep-frying.

You can put all those fears to rest with your Air Fryer. You can have plenty of deep fried and crispy food without compromising on flavor or texture while cutting down on the calories you consume. The recipes that have been mentioned in this book are easy to follow, simple and they will help you in cooking delicious and healthy food. The next time you have your friends or family over for a meal, you can cook them food using your new Air Fryer.

I would like to thank you once again for purchasing this book. All that is left for you to do will be to get started. By making use of the recipes that have been mentioned in this book, you will be able to make the most of your Air Fryer. I am sure you cannot wait to start using your swanky new gadget and whip up delicious and healthy food.

All the best!

And finally… If you liked the book, I would like to ask you to do me the favor of leaving a review on Amazon.

Please go to your account on Amazon, or pastes the link below into your browser.

http://amzn.to/2vhQArh

Thank you very much!

THE END

www.ingramcontent.com/pod-product-compliance
Lightning Source LLC
LaVergne TN
LVHW052302020325
804929LV00011B/1128